BEYOND THE LIMIT

■

ВНЕ ЛИМИТА

BEYOND THE LIMIT

■

ВНЕ ЛИМИТА

■

Poems

■

Irina Ratushinskaya

Translated by Frances Padorr Brent
and Carol J. Avins

■

Northwestern University Press

English translation and notes, foreword, and translator's introduction copyright © 1987 by Frances Padorr Brent and Carol J. Avins.

Russian text copyright © 1987 by Irina Ratushinskaya.

The following poems first appeared in *Formations* in different versions: 12, 13, 14, 37

Grateful acknowledgment is made to Little, Brown and Company for an excerpt from "Requiem," *Poems of Akhmatova*, 1973, translated by Stanley Kunitz with Max Hayward.

Library of Congress Cataloging-in-Publication Data

Ratushinskaĩa, Irina.
    Beyond the limit.

    English and Russian.
    1. Ratushinskaĩa, Irina—Translations, English.
I. Brent, Frances Padorr.   II. Avins, Carol.   III. Title.
PG 3485.5.A875A6   1987   891.71'44   87-5767
ISBN 0-8101-0748-1
ISBN 0-8101-0749-X (pbk.)

Acknowledgments

THE RUSSIAN typescript of *Beyond the Limit* was first presented to us in the spring of 1985 when Irina Ratushinskaya was in camp ZhKh 385/3-4 in Barashevo. The manuscript contained an epigraph and forty-one poems, conceived of as a single book, dated, and titled by the author. Six poems (15, 43, 44, 45, 46, 47), not included in any of the samizdat typescripts, belonged in this collection as well, and so they were sent to us after the poet arrived in England. Five are undated. There are several people who provided us with help and encouragement and they deserve our special thanks. Michael Heim, Anna Linden, Gary Saul Morson, and Boris Pokrovsky read the Russian text and English translations in various stages, offering suggestions and clarifications which were invaluable. Philip Balla, who was then assistant executive director of the PEN American Center, was generous with his time and resources. Yefim Kotlyar's determination to make the world aware of Ratushinskaya's work and her fate has been profoundly enlightening.

It is fitting for this work to include the names of several women prisoners of conscience who served with Ratushinskaya: Jadvyga Bieliauskiene, Galina Barats-Kokhan, Lydia Lasmane-Doronina, Olha Heiko Matusevich, Lagle Parek, Natalya Lazareva, Raisa Rudenko, Tatyana Velikanova, and Tatyana Osipova.

v

Содержание

Contents

ix

Foreword

AKHMATOVA'S "Requiem" begins with a cameo scene outside Leningrad's prison lines during the Yezhov terror: a woman dazed from suffering, her lips blue from cold, overhears the poet's name in the crowd and whispers,

> "Can you describe this?"
> And I said: "I can."
> Then something like a smile passed fleetingly over what had once been her face.

The great poets of the Soviet era have stood as chroniclers of loss and affliction. Akhmatova understood this thoroughly when she wrote her famous lyric on Lot's wife who crystallizes a series of contradictions. How does one look back at what can no longer exist? How does one survive and remember? How does one see and survive?

> How we come to resemble—
> in gaze, brow, corners of mouth—our husbands.
> How we remember them—down to the vein of skin—
> torn away for years,
> how we write: "It's not so terrible . . . "

The text is Irina Ratushinskaya's and her lyrics are derived from the age-old concerns of love, separation, and memory but history has placed her solidly in the Soviet tradition as well. She asks, "How can we be capable of such things—?" and her poetry concentrates on the inventory: signal apparatus, the prison camp cot, and betrayal. There is also delirium: coldness, oscillating specters of escape, imagined and anthropomorphized animal companions. The poems are a gesture against oppression and the subordination of the individual; they register outrage and record what survives.

Sometimes the controversy surrounding the obscurity or prestige of our English-speaking poets seems unbearably paltry. In his excellent lecture on this subject many years ago, Randall Jarrell reminded us, "The poet writes his poem for its own sake, for the sake of that order of things in which the poem takes the place that has awaited it." The poet writes because she is completing a natural destiny of things; Ratushinskaya would agree with this. After her education was ostensibly complete she happened to read the work of Mandelstam, Tsvetaeva, and Pasternak and she experienced it as a series of shocks connecting her to "all the pent up notions of who I might have been"—this included as well a new understanding of her Polish ancestry. The events of Ratushinskaya's life give testimony to the fact that it is not so simple when one's obligation to the "order of things" has to be paid for.

What we know of Ratushinskaya's trial and sojourn in the Gulag comes to us primarily from legal documents and various reports issued by monitoring committees including Amnesty International and PEN International. In 1985, a diary kept by inmates of Zone 4 (the "strict regime" camp for women prisoners of conscience) was smuggled to the west; the entries, recorded by Ratushinskaya, were corroborated by witnesses or prisoners who had been released.*

In March of 1983, when she was twenty-nine years old, Ratushinskaya was charged with the following offenses: "authorship of poetry, documents in defense of human rights, and articles concerning the Polish labor movement published in the bulletin of SMOT (Free Interprofessional Union of Workers); the possession of anti-Soviet literature (which included the works of the poet Voloshin, d. 1932); and oral agitation and propaganda."** Her trial lasted only three days. The lawyer chosen by Ratushinskaya and her relatives was denied the right to see her files or attend the hearings. When Ratushinskaya asked for permission to defend herself, the presiding judge refused. Friends and family members were not allowed in the courtroom. A lawyer assigned to the case acted contrary to the defendant's interest, at the end of the trial requesting an acquittal only because "Ratushinskaya did not succeed in convincing anyone of the validity of her slanderous beliefs and no one followed her on the path of crime." Ratushinskaya was never given the original document of sentence so that it was legally impossible to draft an appeal. On 5 March 1983, she was sentenced to seven years of hard labor to be followed by five years of internal exile, the harshest punishment a woman political prisoner has received since the Stalinist period.

*"Khronika barashevskoi (politicheskoi zhenskoi) zony" [Chronicle of the Barashevo (women political prisoners) zone], *Materialy samizdata* 17 (20 May 1985).

**Aleksandr Aloits, "Ugolovnoe delo Iriny Ratushinskoi" [Violations of Soviet law in the case of Irina Ratushinskaya], *Novoe russkoe slovo* (24 June 1986).

Ratushinskaya was deported in April 1983 to Zone 4 of corrective labor camp number 3 at Barashevo, the only known settlement for women political prisoners—"especially dangerous state criminals." The camp is part of the larger Dubrovlag network built during the Stalin era and it permits the harshest conditions for women prisoners allowable under Soviet law. In the summer of 1983, daily life in the camp grew perceptibly more brutal and the women were served constantly with irrational and humiliating regulations. They were given badges to wear on their breasts and arms identifying them with their crime and length of sentence. The prison warden demanded they stand when she entered the room and insisted that they address her as "citizen superintendent." They were told to wear boots even during the hottest days of the year and were forbidden to leave their sewing machines during work hours. The women were goaded by guards: "How are you going to have children after a spell in solitary?" For staging work strikes or insulting guards they were sent to isolation (shizo) for up to fifteen days at a time where confinement and coldness in the winter months worsened their health. The isolation cell contained four sleeping boards which were drawn up during the day like beds in a Pullman car, four small chairs, a radiator which seldom worked, and a large slop bucket chained to the wall. The floor consisted of loosely spaced wooden planks which covered a slab of cement about forty centimeters thick. The windows were barred but seldom held glass. With a smuggled thermometer, temperatures in the winter were measured as low as eight degrees Celsius (forty-six degrees Fahrenheit). Meals of solid food were permitted on alternate days. During the day all bedding was removed and prisoners were allowed to wear only thin dresses; stockings and heavier work clothes were confiscated. Instead of boots, they were given slippers which had already been worn by other inmates and carried infection.

It was in the solitude of shizo that most of the poems from *Beyond the Limit* were written with a sharpened matchstick on a bar of soap. When they were memorized, the poet washed her hands and the palimpsest was erased. The poems were composed sporadically over a period of fourteen months at the same time that Ratushinskaya was consumed in the chaos and humiliations of the camp: letters were confiscated, visits were denied, a vegetable garden the prisoners had planted was dug up by the guards and destroyed. In August Ratushinskaya participated in a sustained hunger strike, protesting the harsh treatment of two older women. After seven days all fasting prisoners were isolated in the infirmary and on the eighth day they were force-fed. Ratushinskaya resisted and so she was handcuffed and force-fed by six men. In the commotion they struck her head against the frame of a trestle bed and then poured liquid down her throat while she was unconscious. Afterwards, she was placed in a psychiatric cell with no natural light or ventilation. When she revived she had symptoms of a concussion but was not given medical attention. During the autumn she continued to suffer from pain in the region of her kidneys, fever, high blood pressure, and a heart condition, but she participated in hunger strikes and was placed in the isolation cell on numerous occasions. In December, Ratushinskaya shared a punishment cell with Natalya Lazareva, who had served a previous sentence in the camp. Over a period of five days, Lazareva suffered several heart attacks and an inflamed appendix. When Ratushinskaya called for help, a nurse through the serving hatch said the prisoner's urinalysis was "excellent" and so the doctors would not come. On New Year's Eve, Ratushinskaya comforted the writhing woman who lay on the floor; the radiators didn't work. At night she recited poems to the criminal prisoners in adjacent cells.

These poems have the perilous task of transforming loss into memory and love. "Nothing is mine! Just as you have no one, nothing!" she writes, echoing the poets who have come before her for they share this most ordinary reason for being: to confront the necessities of a disordered world and to describe what has happened before it is gone.

Frances Padorr Brent

Translator's Introduction

LITERARY HISTORY records many disputes about the degree to which poetry is translatable. It is beyond dispute, however, that to translate a poem is to transform it—sometimes into a creation that bears some kinship to the original, sometimes into a creature of a distant species.

One of us is a specialist in Russian literature; the other is a poet who does not know Russian. Working from my rough translation, Frances Padorr Brent made another draft; each poem was then jointly deliberated and revised. The translations follow the Russian closely. Where we have deviated slightly from the letter of the original (by changing some line breaks and accomodating ambiguity and idiom, for example), it has been with the aim of creating an English poem that renders the complexity and poetic sensibility conveyed to the reader of the Russian. We have tried to emerge from the translation process with a voice that is recognizably Ratushinskaya's, but the voice heard by readers of the English is inevitably in a different cadence, a different pitch, than that of the poet herself. The following comments may serve to narrow the distance between the experience of reading the original and reading the translation—to help the reader perceive, if not retrieve, what is transformed in translation.

One basic and often-noted distinction between contemporary Russian and English-language poetry is the greater traditionalism of Russian poets in the use of rhyme and meter. Ratushinskaya's poems, like most in the modern Russian tradition, are rhymed; many are metrically regular. They are at the same time richly varied in form and in tone. Some literary works grounded in the experience of imprisonment convey monotony; this cycle, the product of a young poet-prisoner's experience and experiments in verse, reveals the multifaceted nature both of labor camp existence and of the poet's talent.

Within the cycle, archaisms and ancient settings mingle with the language of labor camp jargon, philosophical musing, dissident's challenge, prophesy, and fairy tale. Some poems approach the rhythms of conversation; in others the poet exploits a regular rhyme scheme and meter to serve her purpose. The sonorous anapestic lines of "Now the dance on the deep blue flames is done" cast the spell of a hypnotic incantation. In the poem that follows ("I'm sitting on the floor, leaning against the radiator") the poet modulates to lines looser in form, to a more conversational voice. Other adjacent poems show a comparable range: the measured, troubled homage of "Like Mandelstam's swallow" yields to the fairy-tale tone and whimsy of "I'll take out a big trunk." This storybook singsong—used to poignant effect in a poem like "I'll drop all that I'm doing"—might be placed at one end of Ratushinskaya's register. A quite different point on that register is occupied by one of the more complex poems, "Our conscience has two inflections." Here the poet shows her force with the insistent beat of words paired by sound and sense that is reminiscent of Marina Tsvetaeva—another poet of broad range and woman of powerful voice.

Ratushinskaya shares with the poets of Tsvetaeva's generation—those who came to adulthood around the Russian Revolution—and with earlier literary predecessors a sense of the close link between her personal experience and the national history of which she is a part. These poems are not limited by their datelines, and they are seen too narrowly if read only as individual portrait. One is aware, from the opening lines, of the interpenetration of personal and communal, past and present.

Beyond the Limit opens with a four-line epigraph—a poem that echoes the rhythmic and syntactic form of the Old Russian epic song, thus signaling that the reader is being brought into a chronicle of a historical—and historic—time. What time, and whose? To a non-Russian reader, the "Red Square" named in the opening line denotes only the present-day locale of patriotic displays; given the folk-poetry ring of the line, the Russian reader may see superimposed the site of an era when tsars still lived in the Kremlin.

For the most part, though, Ratushinskaya's linking of past and present is not muted by translation. The poem beginning "They're forming columns down below," for example, interweaves on the field of action gilded armor and bullets, tanks and centurions' cloaks. This surrealistic, hallucinatory vision of history makes it plain that we perceive the present through our knowledge of the past—that the present for us is a superimposition of past eras.

Language, for any culture, is the most basic guarantee of historical continuity. "Our conscience has two inflections," which follows the epigraph, is one poem in which the Russian language plays center stage. A prerevolutionary feature of Russian orthography, "exiled" from usage, serves here as an emblem of a suppressed but potential way of being. Ratushinskaya develops an opposition between properties of language that come to represent properties of self, of conscience—the malleable, conciliatory side versus the proscribed side that is hidden from view. The tension between them is summed up in the final line, in one word whose meanings extend beyond the translators' "doublevoicedness."

The Russian *dvuxgolosie*, with its twin form *dvoeglasie*, is first of all a musical term denoting two-part singing; in liturgical usage, it refers to the two-part chanting of a service. This meaning, however, is canceled by the word's other sense—not the harmonious blending of voices, but their discordant clash. Harmony and dissonance—or, to move beyond the musical context, dissidence—are doubles. The Russian word not mentioned but implied means literally "single-voicedness"; it is the common word for unanimity, *edinoglasie*. Not this, but doublevoicedness, prevails in the poem. For all the grimness of the experience that gave rise to this cycle, Ratushinskaya's stance is essentially hopeful. This poem, among others, suggests that the voices of our consciousness which are part of the legacy of the past will continue to resonate, in the poet's phrase, "through an abyss of years."

That the voice of Ratushinskaya has reached us in her own time is one justification for the hopefulness her poems express. Osip Mandelstam, one of the poets to whom Ratushinskaya acknowledges a debt, wrote in an early essay that while prose is written for a contemporary audience, poetry "always addresses a more or less distant, unknown addressee, in whose existence the poet cannot doubt, without doubting in himself." Ratushinskaya, who had only precarious links to the outside during the period when she composed these poems, must nonetheless have been confident of finding that eventual reader whom Mandelstam terms a "providential interlocutor." She explicitly engaged in dialogue with this audience even from within the camp, addressing one poem, "To My Unknown Friend, David McGolden," to a well-wisher whose letter had somehow been delivered to her. Others in her audience ensured that Ratushinskaya's half of the dialogue would in turn be transmitted to the rest of us on what she calls "the other half of this sphere."

Carol J. Avins

BEYOND THE LIMIT

■

ВНЕ ЛИМИТА

As across Red Square the flags careen,
a rabble of birds screams, circling above the rampart...
They've brought us to allegiance by deceit.
But it's not so — I never vowed.

———————————

Как по площади по Красной рыщут флаги
Птичья чернь орет, кружа над валом . . .
Нас обманом привели к присяге.
Но неправда — я не присягала.

I

Есть у нашей совести два оттенка,
Два молчания, две стороны застенка.
Сколько лет старались забыть! Однако
В алфавите два молчаливых знака:
Мягкий—круглый, родственный и лояльный,
И старинный твердый, ныне опальный.
Сколько раз его, гордого, запрещали,
Из машинок выламывали клещами,
Заменяли апострофом, и у слов
Обрубали концы, чтоб ни-ни! Крылом,
Лебедь стриженный, не зачерпнешь утра,
Не почувствуешь осенью, что пора,
В холода высот не рванешь из жил—
Захлебнешься сном, не узнав, что жил.
И споют тебе колыбельный гимн
Медным горлышком, чтоб на страх другим!
Самиздатский томик—в архивный тлен—
Крысьей лапкой на склизком листать столе,
Мягкой пылью—тише!—стелить шажок,
И—шнурок на вдох: помолчи, дружок!
Помолчи—проси
Не губить—простить,
Помолчи—скажи
Слово—и спаси
Сам себя! Во лжи—
Хочешь?—Воскреси
Униженьем—жизнь!
Ну?! И—хруст в кости.
Но старинной твердости взгляд—ответ,
Голубых кровей отраженный свет,
Гул молчания—княжьего—палачу—
Ни полслова! С телеги—толпе—молчу!
Как суду—ни бровью, так им—ни стон,
Ни холопский—в четыре конца—поклон!

I.

Our conscience has two inflections,
two silences, two sides of the torture chamber.
How many years have we tried to forget? However,
in the alphabet there are two silent signs:
the soft—round, kindred and loyal—
and the hard one, from former times, now in disgrace.
How often the proud one's been forbidden,
ripped from typewriters with pincers,
replaced by an apostrophe, and words—
their endings lopped, so *no-no! absolutely not!*
With your wing,
clipped swan, you will not scoop the morning,
will not sense in autumn that it's time;
into coldness of heights, you will not burst, straining—
but choke in sleep, not knowing that you lived.
And they will sing you a lullaby-hymn,
bronze-throated, so others will be warned!
Little samizdat volume—into archival decomposition—
to be leafed by a rat's paw on the slimy table,
like soft dust—*hush!* to lay a silent step.
And—lacing breath back: *be quiet, friend!*
Be quiet—beg
not for ruin—but pardon—
be quiet—say
a word—and save
yourself! In falsehood—
do you want—humbled—
to resurrect—life!
Well? And—cracking of bone.
But the gaze of a past era's steadfastness is an answer,
reflected light of blue-bloods,
roar of silence—princely—for the executioner—
not a half-word! From the cart—to the crowd—I'm silent!
As to the court—not an eyebrow, so to them—not a moan,
nor a slavish—to-four-sides—bow!

3

Привыкать ли: с закинутой головой
К эшафоту—под радостный зверий вой,
Четкой поступью—медленно—по плевкам,
Да по грязной соломе, да по векам;
Не оправдываясь—не пристанет ложь!—
Той же смертной дорогой и ты пройдешь,
И российской совестью—в прорву лет—
Двухголосье молчания грянет вслед.

—3 июня 1983

Should you grow accustomed—with head tossed back,
to the scaffold—to the accompaniment of joyous animal howl,
sure-footed—slowly—through the spittle,
and on dirty straw, through ages
without justifying yourself—falsehood won't stick to you!
Along that same fatal road you too will pass,
and as the Russian conscience—through an abyss of years—
the doublevoicedness of silence will ring after.

—3 June 1983

2.

А я не знаю, как меня убьют:
Пристрелят ли в начале заварухи—
И я прижму растерянные руки
К дыре, где было сердце.
И сошьют
Мне белую легенду, и примерят,
И нарядят—потом уже, потом,
Когда окончится! Когда сочтут потери,
Протопят каждый уцелевший дом,
И вдруг смутятся, затворяя двери,
И загрустят, неведомо о ком.
А может даже раньше—хоть сейчас:
Разденут—и в бетон, в окmoчененье
Законное! За подписью врача—
В калеки, в смертники—на обученье!
Чтобы не дрогнув—медленно—до дна!
Согласно предписаниям режима!
О, белая легенда! Холодна!
И—с головы до пят—неотторжима!
А может, проще—новостью в письме:
—Ты знаешь . . . Оказалось . . . Что ж, мужайся!
Ты сильная . . . И удержу ли смех
Над смятыми листками? Как прижаться
Дырой, где было сердце—только что—
К рукам—уже ненужным и неважным?
И дальше—как? За гранью? За чертой
Непреступаемой? Отмеренной? Бумажной?
Ох, только бы не так! Не через вас,
Мои! Пускай не вы, пускай другие!
Ведь не пощады! Но другую гибель—
Цемент ли, пуля!—Только не слова!
А впрочем, что я горожу? Не мне—
В друзьях сомненье допустить, в любимом—
Смятенье допустить! Единым «нет»—
Я отметаю допущенье грима

2.

And I don't know how they'll kill me:
whether they'll shoot me at that point when chaos starts
and I'll press my trembling hands to the hole that was my heart
and they'll sew me a white legend, fitting it,
to array me—at that point, then,
when it's over! When they count their losses,
they'll begin warming each house that's intact
and suddenly grow troubled, shutting doors,
fall sad, not knowing for whom.
And maybe before that—even right now:
they'll undress me—and into concrete, into lawful
stiffness! By the signature of a doctor—
send me to the crippled, the condemned,—so they'll teach me!
Without faltering—to go slowly—to the bottom
as regimen prescribes!
Oh, white legend! You're cold!
And—from head to toes—unseizable!
And maybe, simply—in the form of a letter's news:
—*You see . . . It turns out . . . Well, take courage . . .*
We know you're strong . . . And how can I hold back my laughter
at those crumpled pages? How can one press
a hole, where just now there was a heart—
one's hands—already unneeded, unimportant?
And after that—how? Beyond the limit? Beyond the border
that cannot be crossed? Measured? On paper?
Oh, any way but that! Not through you,
my own! Don't let it be you, but others!
Not mercy but a different death—
cement or bullet—Only not words!
Anyway, why am I chattering? That's not for me—
to assume doubt in my friends, my beloved—
to admit uncertainty! No is my only answer—
I refuse the assumption of greasepaint

На самых верных душах всей земли,
На самых яростных и самых гордых!
Что, волчий век? Воротишь зверью морду?
Кому кого бояться—знаешь?
Пли!

—15 июля 1983

on the most loyal in all the land,
most fierce, proud!
Well, what is it, wolf-life century? Curling
your snout like a beast?
Who's to be afraid of whom—do you know?
Fire!

—15 July 1983

3.

Татьяне Великановой

Неумелая пила,
Пышные опилки.
Предосенние дела.
Доживем до ссылки!
Скоро, скоро на этап,
В теплый свитер—скоро,
А свобода—по пятам
С матерщиной пополам,
Сыском да надзором!
Восемьдесят третий год—
Солью, не хлебами—
Вхруст по косточкам пройдет,
Переломится вот-вот!
Недорасхлебали
За ворота, за предел—
С каждой нотой выше!
Тихий ангел отлетел.
Нам судьба накрутит дел—
Дайте только выжить!
Ну, до встречи где-нибудь.
Зэковское счастье—
Улыбнись!
Счастливый путь.
Нету сил прощаться.

—1 сентября 1983

10

3.

For Tatyana Velikanova

Clumsy saw,
abundant filings.
Pre-autumn's matters.
We'll make it till exile!
Soon, to the transport—
in a warm sweater—soon,
as for freedom, on its heels
half-mixed with cursing,
with tracking, surveillance!
This eighty-third year—
with salt, not bread—
will pass into a cracking of bones—
just at the point of breaking!
Still unsolved—
beyond the gates, beyond the boundary—
with every note higher!
Quiet angel takes wing.
Fate will twist matters for us—
may we only survive!
Well, till we meet somewhere—
zek's happiness—
smile!
A good journey.
No strength to say good-bye.

—1 September 1983

4.

Что-то завтра, кораблик наш, Малая зона,
Что сбудется нам?
По какому закону—
Скорлупкой по мертвым волнам?
Весь в заплатах и шрамах,
На слове—на честном—одном—
Чьей рукою храним наш кораблик,
Наш маленький дом?
Кто из нас доплывет, догребет, доживет—
До других,
Пусть расскажет: мы знали
Касание этой руки.

—18 сентября 1983

4.

Some tomorrow, little ship of ours, Lesser Zone,
what will become of us?
By what law—
our fragile shell crosses dead waves?
All in patches and scars,
on a word—honest—single—
whose hand preserves our little ship,
little house?
Which of us will sail, will row to shore, will live—
reaching others,
let him tell: we knew
the touch of that hand.

—18 September 1983

5.

Если выйти из вечера прямо в траву,
По асфальтовым трещинам—в сумрак растений,
То исполнится завтра же—и наяву
Небывалое лето счастливых знамений.
Все приметы—к дождю,
Все дожди—на хлеба,
И у всех почтальонов—хорошие вести.
Всем кузнечикам—петь,
А творцам—погибать
От любви к сотворенным—красивым, как песни.
И тогда, и тогда—
Опадет пелена,
И восторженным зреньем—иначе, чем прежде,—
Недошедшие письма прочтем,
И сполна
Недоживших друзей оправдаем надежды.
И подымем из пепла
Наш радостный дом,
Чтобы встал вдохновенно и неколебимо.
Как мы счастливы будем—когда-то потом!
Как нам нужно дожить!
Ну не нам—так любимым.

—3 октября 1983

5.

If one could go out from evening straight onto grass,
along asphalt cracks—into a dusk of green-growth,
then it would come to pass, tomorrow—and wide awake,
imagined summer of happy portents.
All signs—towards rain,
all rains—for bread,
and all postmen carrying good news.
All crickets shall sing,
and creators—perish
out of love for the created—beautiful as songs.
And then, and then—
scales will fall
and with rapturous vision—different from before—
we shall read letters that never were delivered,
justify hopes of unsurviving friends.
And we'll raise from ashes
our joyous house,
so it will stand, shining, unshakable.
How happy we shall be—sometime after!
How we need to live on!
And if not—then our loved ones.

—3 October 1983

6.

Дай мне кличку, тюрьма,
В этот первый апрель,
В этот вечер печали,
С тобой разделенный.
В этот час твоих песен
О зле и добре,
Да любовных признаний,
Да шуток соленых.
У меня отобрали
Друзей и родных,
Крест сорвали с цепочки
И сняли одежду,
А потом сапогами
Лупили под дых,
Выбивая с пристрастьем
Остатки надежды.
Мое имя подшито—
И профиль, и фас—
В нумерованном деле.
Под стражей закона—
Ничего моего!
Так же, как и у вас
Никого, ничего!
На решетке оконной—
Вот я весь—окрести,
Дай мне имя, тюрьма,
Проводи на этап
Не мальчишку, а зэка,
Чтоб встречала меня
Потеплей Колыма,
Место ссылок и казней
Двадцатого века.

—5 октября 1983

6.

Give me a nickname, prison,
this first April
evening of sadness
shared with you.
This hour for your songs
of evil and goodness,
confessions of love,
salty jokes.
They've taken my friends,
ripped the cross from its chain,
torn clothes,
and then with boots
struck at my breastbone
torturing the remains
of hope.
My name is filed
in profile, full-face—
a numbered dossier.
In custody—
nothing is mine!
Just as you have
no one, nothing!
On the window's grating
here's all of me—christen me,
give me a name, prison,
send off to the transport
not a boy, but a zek,
so I'll be welcomed
with endearments by Kolyma,
place of outcasts, executions
in this twentieth century.

—5 October 1983

7.

Что ты помнишь о нас, мой печальный,
Посылая мне легкие сны?
Чем ты бредишь пустыми ночами,
Когда стены дыханью тесны?
Вспоминаешь ли первые встречи,
Дальний стан, перекрестки веков?
Говорит ли неведомой речью
Голубое биенье висков?
Помнишь варваров дикое стадо,
И на гребне последней стены
Мы—последние—держим осаду,
И одною стрелой сражены?
Помнишь дерзкий побег на рассвете,
Вдохновенный озноб беглецов,
И кудрявый восточный ветер,
Мне закидывающий лицо?
Я не помню, была ли погоня,
Но наверно отстала вдали,
И морские веселые кони
Донесли нас до теплой земли.
Помнишь странное синее платье—
И ребенок под шалью затих . . .
В этот год исполнялось проклятье,
И кому-то кричали: «Мы—братья!»
А кого-то вздымали на штык . . .
Как тогда мы друг друга теряли—
В суматохе, в дорожной пыли—
И не знали: на день, навсегда ли?
И опять—узнаешь ли—нашли!
Через смерть, через годы и годы,
Через новых рождений черты,
Сквозь забвения темные воды,
Сквозь решетку шепчу: это ты!

—8 октября 1983

7.

What do you recall of us, my sad one,
sending such light dreams?
What fills your delirium on empty nights,
when walls are close with breathing?
Do you remember our first meetings,
far away camp, crossroads of aeons?
Does a pale blue throbbing of the temples
speak an unfathomable language?
Do you remember the wild band of barbarians,
and at the crest of that final wall
we—the last ones—hold the siege,
and with an arrow are struck down?
Do you remember the reckless flight at daybreak,
inspired feverishness of fugitives,
curling eastwind
pounding my face from all sides?
I don't recall if there was a chase,
but probably they fell far behind,
and gay seahorses
carried us to a warm land.
Do you remember a strange deep blue dress—
and the child under a shawl grew quiet . . .
A curse was fulfilled that year,
and to some they cried, "We are brothers!"
and raised some on a bayonet . . .
then we lost each other—
in the turmoil, roadway dust—
And didn't know: for a day, or forever?
And again—do you recognize . . . found each other!
Across death, across years and years,
across markings of new births,
through dark waters of oblivion,
through the grate I whisper: it's you!

—8 October 1983

8.

Помню брошенный храм под Москвою:
Двери настежь, и купол разбит.
И, дитя заслоняя рукою,
Богородица тихо скорбит—
Что у мальчика ножки босые,
А опять впереди холода,
Что так страшно по снегу России—
Навсегда—неизвестно куда—
Отпускать темноглазое чадо,
Чтоб и в этом народе—распять . . .
—Не бросайте каменья, на надо!
Неужели опять и опять—
За любовь, за спасенье и чудо,
За открытый бестрепетный взгляд—
Здесь найдется российский Иуда,
Повторится российский Пилат?
А у нас, у вошедших,—ни крика,
Ни дыхания—горло свело:
По ее материнскому лику
Процарапаны битым стеклом
Матерщины корявые буквы!
И младенец глядит, как в расстрел:
—Ожидайте, Я скоро приду к вам!
В вашем северном декабре
Обожжет Мне лицо, но кровавый
Русский путь Я пройду до конца,
Но спрошу вас—из силы и славы:
Что вы сделали с домом Отца?
И стоим перед Ним изваянно,
По подобию сотворены,
И стучит нам в виски, окаянным,
Ощущение общей вины.
Сколько нам—на крестах и на плахах—
Сквозь пожар материнских тревог—
Очищать от позора и праха

8.

I remember an abandoned church near Moscow:
doors wide open, cupola smashed.
And shielding the infant with her arm
the Virgin quietly mourns. Cold lies ahead,
the boy's feet are bare,
it's frightening across the Russian snow—
Forever, not knowing where—
to let down the child, black-
eyed, among these people, to crucify . . .
Don't throw stones! Don't!
Can it be, once again,
for love, salvation, miracle,
a wide, untrembling gaze—
a Russian Judas will come?
a Russian Pilate will be found?
Among us—those who entered—not a cry
or breath—the throat cramps—
Across his mother's countenance
crooked letters of profanity
scratched with broken glass . . .
The infant gazes as into a fusillade:
Wait—I will come soon,
in your northern December
my face will be scorched
but I will traverse the bloody
Russian path to the end,
and I will ask—out of power and glory—
what have you done with the house of my Father?
And we stand before him, as clay
created in his likeness, cursed,
on our temples: hammering,
sensation of collective guilt.
How long must we—on crosses, executioner's blocks—
through fire of maternal alarms—
cleanse His image of shame,

В нас поруганный образ Его?
Сколько нам отмывать эту землю
От насилия и от лжи?
Внемлешь, Господи? Если внемлешь,
Дай нам силы, чтоб ей служить.

—12 октября 1983

of ashes, scourged within us?
How long wash this earth
of force, falsehood?
Dost thou harken, Lord? If thou dost—
Give us the strength to serve her.

—12 October 1983

9.

Вот и стихли крики, Пенелопа,
Покрывало в сторону!
Он вернулся, твой высоколобый,
К сыну и престолу.
К лошадям своим и горожанам,
К ложу из оливы . . .
Ни разлучница не удержала,
Ни эти, с Олимпа.
Вытер меч, меняя гнев на милость,
Дышит львино . . .
Раз рука его не усумнилась—
Значит, нет невинных!
Всем злодеям вышло наказанье
От законной власти . . .
Вот рабыни смоют кровь с мозаик—
И начнется счастье.

—9 ноября 1983

9.

Now the cries have died down, Penelope,
lay aside your cloth—
He's returned, your lofty-browed one,
to son and throne,
horses and townsmen,
to bed of olive . . .
Neither She-who-separates
nor those from Olympus held him off.
He's wiped his sword, changed mercy to anger,
breathes like a lion . . .
None are innocent
if his hand doesn't falter.
To all who did evil, punishment's meted
from lawful power.
Now the slavewomen wipe blood from mosaics—
and happiness starts.

                              —9 November 1983

10.

Тане и Ване (Осиповой и Ковалеву)

Я проеду страною—
В конвойной свите,
Я измучу людским страданьем глаза,
Я увижу то, что никто не видел—
Но сумею ли рассказать?
Докричу ли, как мы такое можем—
По разлуке, как по водам?
Как становимся мы на мужей похожи—
Взглядом, лбом, уголками рта.
Как мы помним—до каждой прожилки кожи—
Их, оторванных на года,
Как мы пишем им: «не беда,
Мы с тобою—одно и то же,
Не разнять!»
И звучит в ответ
Твердью кованное «навек»—
То стариннейшее из словес,
За которым—без тени—свет.
Я пройду этапом,
Я все запомню—
Наизусть—они не смогут отнять!
Как мы дышим—
Каждый вдох вне закона!
Чем мы живы—
До завтрашнего дня.

—12 ноября 1983

10.

For Tanya Osipova and Vanya Kovalev

I will cross the land—
in a convoy,
exhaust my eyes with sufferings,
see what no one has seen—
but will I be able to give it words?
Will my cry penetrate, how can we be capable
of such things—
across partings, as across waters?
How we come to resemble—
in gaze, brow, corners of mouth—our husbands.
How we remember them—down to the vein of skin—
torn away for years,
how we write: "It's not so terrible . . ."
You and I are one,
impossible to separate!
And an answer sounds
forged in earth—"forever"—
that most venerable of words,
beyond which—and shadowless—is light.
I will pass through in convoy,
commit it all—
to memory—they won't take it away!
How we breathe—
each breath outside law.
What we stay alive by—
until tomorrow.

—12 November 1983

И доживу, и выживу, и спросят:
Как били головою о топчан,
Как приходилось мерзнуть по ночам,
Как пробивалась молодая проседь . . .
Но улыбнусь. И что-нибудь сострю
И отмахнусь от набежавшей тени.
И честь воздам сухому сентябрю,
Который стал моим вторым рожденьем.
И спросят: не болит ли вспоминать,
Не обманувшись легкостью наружной.
Но грянут в памяти былые имена—
Прекрасные—как старое оружие.
И расскажу о лучших всей земли,
О самых нежных, но непобедимых,
Как провожали, как на пытку шли,
Как ждали писем от своих любимых.
И спросят: что нам помогало жить,
Когда ни писем, ни вестей—лишь стены,
Да холод камеры, да чушь казенной лжи,
Да тошные посулы за измену.
И расскажу о первой красоте,
Которую увидела в неволе.
Окно в морозе! Ни глазков, ни стен,
И ни решеток, и ни долгой боли—
Лишь синий свет на крохотном стекле,
Витой узор—чудесней не приснится!
Ясней взгляни—и расцветут смелей
Разбойничьи леса, костры и птицы!
И сколько раз бывали холода,
И сколько окон с той поры искрилось—
Но никогда уже не повторилось
Такое буйство радужного льда!
Да и за что бы это мне—сейчас,
И чем бы этот праздник был заслужен?

II.

I'll live through this, survive, and they'll ask me:
how they beat my head on the prison cot,
how it froze during the nights,
how the first wisps of gray hair broke through.
I'll smile and say some joke,
wave away the shadow that comes quickly,
and I'll honor the dry September
that's become my second birth.
And they'll ask: doesn't it hurt to remember?
without being deceived by the lightness around?
But names from the past burst in my memory—
beautiful—like old weapons.
And I'll tell about the best in all the world,
the most tender, who don't break,
how they accompanied us, how they went to torture,
awaited letters from those they loved.
And they'll ask: what helped us live,
without letters or news—just walls
and coldness in the cell, stupidity of official lies,
nauseating promises for betrayal.
And I'll tell about the first beauty which I saw in this captivity:
window in the frost! No spy holes, nor walls,
nor grating—no long suffering—
only bluish light in the smallest glass.
Whirling pattern—you can't dream of anything more enchanted!
Look close, you'll see it begin to blossom even more:
forests of thieves, fires, birds!
and how many times there was coldness
and how many windows glistened from that time on.
But it hasn't happened again,
such violence of prism-ice,
and why should it be mine—now,
and what have I done to deserve this holiday?

Такой подарок может быть лишь раз.
А может быть, один лишь раз и нужен.

—30 ноября 1983

Such a gift can happen only once.
Perhaps one needs it only once.

—30 November 1983

12.

Вот и снова декабрь
Расстилает холсты,
И узорчатым хрустом
Полны мостовые
И напрасно хлопочут
Четыре стихии
Уберечь нас от смертной
Его чистоты.
Пустим наши планеты
По прежним кругам—
Видно, белая нам
Выпадает дорога.
Нашу линию жизни
Залижут снега—
Но еще нам осталось
Пройти эпилогом.
Но, упрямых следов
Оставляя печать,
Подыматься по мерзлым ступеням
До плахи—
И суровую холодность
Чистой рубахи
Ощутить благодатью
На слабых плечах.

— декабрь 1983 (?)

12.

Here is December again
spreading canvases
and with its patterned crunch
roadways fill
and the four elements
are hopeless to try
saving us from its mortal
purity.
We'll let our planets
out to their previous circles—
it seems a white road
falls to our lot.
Our lifelines will be licked
by snow—
but it's left for us
to go along
like an epilogue.

But leaving the stamp
of stubborn footprints
to rise on frozen steps
to the executioner's block—
and the severe cold
of a clean shirt
falls like grace
on weak shoulders.

—December 1983 (?)

13.

Вот и кончена пляска по синим огням,
По каленым орешкам углей.
Вот и роздых оранжевым пылким коням,
А тепло все смуглей и смуглей.
Оскудевшей ладошкой остатки лови—
Не держи—отпускай на скаку!
Остыванье камина печальней любви,
Обреченней котенка в снегу.
А когда догорит, отлетит и умрет,
Как цыганский костер на песке—
То останется маленький грустный зверек,
Охвативший колени в тоске.
Что ж, не все танцевать этой долгой зимой,
Раз никак не кончается год!
И теряется в сумерках тоненький вой,
Унесенный в пустой дымоход.
Что ж, не все баловаться, свиваясь кольцом,
Да хвостом разводить вензеля . . .
И хотелось бы года с хорошим концом—
Да остыла под лапкой зола . . .
Не скули, дурачок, мы газету зажжем—
Всю подшивку—в разбойничий дым!
Хоть и мало тепла—да горит хорошо!
Потанцуем, а там поглядим.

—3 декабря 1983

13.

Now the dance on the deep blue flames is done,
on the roasted nuts of coals.
Now a breather for the orange mote-drawn steeds,
and the warmth grows more and more dusky.
Catch the remains with a weakening palm—
don't hold—let them gallop!
A cooling hearth is sadder than love,
more doomed than a cat in snow.
And when it burns down, drifts off and dies,
like a gypsy fire on sand—
there will remain a little downcast beast,
clasping its knees in grief.
Well, one can't dance forever through this long winter,
since the year just refuses to end.
And the thin wail is lost in the twilight,
carried up the empty flue.
Well, one can't fool forever, coiling up in a ring,
giving rise to monograms with one's tail . . .

And I'd like a year with a good ending—
But ashes have cooled under my paw . . .
Don't whimper, silly fool, we'll light a newspaper—
a whole file—up in brigand's smoke!
This warmth is slight—still it burns well!
Let's dance a while, then we'll have a look.

—3 December 1983

14.

Я сижу на полу, прислонясь к батарее,—
Южанка, мерзлячка!
От решетки на лампочке тянутся длинные тени.
Очень холодно.
Хочется сжаться в комок по-цыплячьи.
Молча слушаю ночь,
Подбородок уткнувши в колени.
Тихий гул по трубе,
Может пустят горячую воду!
Но сомнительно.
Климат ШИЗО. Кайнозойская эра.
Кто скорей отогреет—Державина твердая ода,
Марциала опальный привет,
Или бронза Гомера?
Мышка Машка стащила сухарь
И грызет за парашей.
Двухдюймовый грабитель,
Невиннейший жулик на свете.
За окном суета,
И врывается в камеру нашу—
Только что со свободы—
Декабрьский разбойничий ветер.
Гордость Хельсинкской группы не спит—
По дыханию слышу.
В Пермском лагере тоже не спит
Нарушитель режима.
Где-то в Киеве крутит приемник
Другой одержимый . . .
И встает Орион,
И проходит от крыши до крыши.
И печальная повесть России
(А может, нам снится?)
Мышку Машку, и нас, и приемник,
И свет негасимый—
Умещает на чистой, еще непочатой странице,

14.

I'm sitting on the floor, leaning against the radiator,
Southerner, easy-to-touch-with-frost.
Long shadows are stretched from the grating on the lamp;
it's very cold.
I wish I could shrink in a clot like a chick.
Silently, I listen to the night,
bury my chin in my knees.
Quiet buzz in the pipe.
Maybe they'll switch on the hot water—
but it's doubtful.
Shizo climate. Cenozoic era.
Who'll warm me up faster—Derzhavin's firm ode,
Martial's dishonored greeting,
bronze Homer?
Mouse Mashka stole a crust of bread
behind the can and gnaws on it.
Two-inch thief!
Most innocent cheater in the world!
There, it's stirring outside the window—
and it bursts into our cell—
just coming from freedom—
December's thieves' wind.
The pride of Helsinki Watch is not asleep—
I hear from the breathing.
Someone who resists
in Perm's camp also doesn't sleep;
somewhere in Kiev, another one, obsessed,
tunes a receiver . . .
And Orion rises,
and passes from roof to roof
and the sad story of Russia
(or maybe we're just dreaming it?)
Mouse Mashka and ourselves and the radio
and the light-never-switched-off—
will arrange on the clean, not yet started page,

Открывая на завтрашний день
Эту долгую зиму.

—16 декабря 1983

opening to tomorrow's day
this long winter.

    —16 December 1983

15.

Таня Осипова, как вы мне надоели!
Даже здесь—вдвоем: близнецовый эффект виноват!
Серый ветер гуляет по дощатой нашей постели.
И вечерние мыши вышли на променад.
Мы опять в шизо, ох не гладят нас по головке!
Под одной звездой отмерзать ото всех забот.
Но на крайний случай, вы в шизо, а я в голодовке.
Или тот же случай, только наоборот.
Видно, ангелы наши время нашли и место
Спохватиться: где мы болтались врозь, и они правы.
Где вы были в Москве во время моих наездов?
И где я была, когда в Лефортово—вы?
Двум таким безголосым как же было не спеться?
От судьбы не уйдешь: раз уж нас не свели свои—
Удружили власти, теперь никуда не деться!
Принесли баланду; возьмите на нас двоих.

—декабрь 1983

15.

Tanya Osipova, I've had enough of you!
Even here—together: the twin effect's to blame!
A gray wind plays across our wood-planked bed
and the evening mice come out for promenade.
Shizo again, no one strokes our heads.
Under only a star, one freezes numb with troubles.
But at the extreme, you're in shizo and I fast—
or the other way around.
Seems our angels have found the time and place
to notice with a start: where we hung around
apart, and they're right.
Where were you when I made those flying trips to Moscow?
And where was I for you in Lefortovo?
How could two such voiceless ones not sing together?
One can't escape fate: friends didn't help us meet—
Those in power brought that favor—can't be undone.
Now they've brought our gruel; take the portions for us both.

—December 1983

16.

Илюше

О чайной ложечке любви
Давай грустить, мой друг далекий!
О том, что бесконечны сроки,
Что так суровы все пророки—
И хоть бы кто благословил!
Мой друг, давай грустить о том,
Как я из марта прибегала,
Ты ждал в дверях.
И в добрый дом
Вводил. И занавес вокзала
Был так нескоро, что цвела
Обломленная наспех ветка—
И в робость воскового света
Каморка тесная плыла.
Давай грустить о том, что мы
Так щедро молоды поныне—
Но нам, рожденным на чужбине
С судьбой скитанья и гордыни,—
Искать ли родины взаймы?
Как онемевший бубенец—
Сердечный спазм.
Сейчас отпустит.
Как впереди бездонно пусто!
Но есть у самой долгой грусти
Одна улыбка под конец.

—30 декабря 1983

16.

For Ilyusha

For a teaspoon of love
let us feel sad, my far off friend!
That terms are endless,
all prophets so severe—
none would give his blessing!
My friend, let's grieve
how I would come running in from March,
you waited in the doorway,
drawing me into that good
house. And the curtain
of the train station was long after that—
so it bloomed:
hastily broken-off branch—
and toward the timidness of the waxy light
the cramped chamber floated.
Let's grieve that we're
so prodigiously young for now—
but must we, born in a foreign place,
fated to wandering, pride,
look for a homeland to borrow?
Like a muted little bell—
a heart spasm.
It will go in a moment.
How bottomlessly empty on ahead!
But in the very longest grief
one smile before the end.

—30 December 1983

17.

A в этом году подуло весной
Четвертого февраля.
И на вспененной лошади вестовой
В нелепом мундире старинных войн
Промчал по мерзлым полям.
Прокатили мускулы облаков
По всем горизонтам гром,
И запели трубы былых полков
Смертью и серебром.
И по грудь в весне провели коней,
И намокли весной плащи,
А что там могло так странно звенеть—
Мне было не различить.
Но рвануло сердце на этот звон,
И усталость крылом смело.
И это был никакой не сон:
Было уже светло.

—4 февраля 1984

17.

This year a spring wind blew
on the fourth of February.
And on the foamed horse, a courier,
in the absurd military jacket
of long-ago soldiers,
tore across frozen fields.
Muscles of clouds rolled by,
on all horizons, thunder,
and the trumpets of past regiments hummed out
death and silver
and they led the steeds up to their chests in spring,
soaked their cloaks in springtime,
but what could have rung so strangely there—
I couldn't make out.
My heart tore at that ringing,
swept away weariness with its wing,
and it was no dream at all.
It was already light.

—4 February 1984

18.

Медвежья песенка

Самым мягким лапкам—
Баю-бай!
Самым круглым попкам—
Баю-бай!
Самым толстопузым,
Теплым и лохматым,
Сонным медвежатам—
Баю-бай!
Как у нас в берлоге
Три бочонка меду,
Как у наших деток—
Сладенькие лапки . . .
Первый сон—гречишный,
А второй—цветочный,
А как выйдет месяц—
Липовый приснится.
Соням и сластенам,
Баловням-задирам,
Медвежовым деткам—
Баюшки под ушко!

—6 февраля 1984

18.

Bear Song

For the softest little paws—
Lullaby!
For the roundest little rumps—
Lullaby!
For the most fat-bellied,
warmest and shaggiest,
sleepiest bear cubs—
Lullaby!
Here in our den,
three little honey pots,
here for our children,
sweetest little paws . . .
    The first dream is of buckwheat—
    the second—flower-blossom,
    and when the moon comes out—
    we'll dream of linden-blossom.
For sleepyheads and sweet tooths,
pets and teases,
little bear cub children,
Lullaby!
little pillows,
to your little ears.

          —6 February 1984

19.

Нарядили в тяжелое платье,
И прекрасною дамой назвали,
И писали с нее Божью матерь,
И клинки на турнирах ломали.
И венцы ей сплетали из лилий,
И потом объявили святой.
И отпели и похоронили—
А она и не знала, за что.

—12 февраля 1984

19.

They arrayed her in heavy dresses,
and called her a fair lady,
and painted the Virgin from her likeness
and broke their lances at tournaments.
And wove her coronals of lilies
and then pronounced her holy.
And chanted her funeral songs, and buried her—
and she was never to know—why.

—12 February 1984

20.

Мы не войдем в одну и ту же реку,
Не разведем заросших берегов,
Не будет нам хромого человека,
Который нас перевезти готов.

А будет вечер—теплый, как настойка
На темных травах; лень и тишина.
Тогда отступит лагерная койка,
И холод камеры, и ветер из окна.

Но мы запомним разговоры в кружку,
Счастливейшие сны в полубреду,
Мордовских баб, пихающих горбушку:
—Хоть хлебушка возьми, не голодуй!

И это нам нести своим любимым,
По-честному делясь—кому о чем:
Все страшное—себе,
Все злое—мимо,
Всю доброту Земли—ему в плечо.

—16 февраля 1984

20.

We will not go into that river
not part the overgrown banks,
for us, there will never be a lame man
prepared to take us across.

But there will be an evening—warm, like an infusion
of warm grasses; lassitude and silence.
Then the prison camp cot will retract
and the cell's coldness, draft from the window.

We'll remember conversation through walls,
happiest dreams in half-delirium.
Mordovian peasant-women, passing us crusts of bread:
—*At least take a bite, don't go hungry!*

And this is for us to bring our loved ones,
honestly dividing—what for whom:
all that terrifies—to ourselves,
all evil—past us,
all goodness of the earth—for his shoulder.

—16 February 1984

21.

Так за дверью: «Вам телеграмма»—
Что б там ни было—открывай!
Так юродивые при храмах—
Чьих пророков хрипят слова?
Так условленное судно
Тем ли парусом обожжет?
В самых долгих минутах судеб
Мы не ведаем, что нас ждет.
Нам не следует знать, что будет,
Но тем тверже мы предстоим,
Вслух настаивая на чуде,
Что положено нам двоим.
По режиму! По праву крови!
И по каждому вздоху врозь!
И по каждой ночи без крова!
И по бреду под стук колес!
Не награда и не возмездье,
Но суровейшее из чудес,
За которым уходят в песню,
Оставляя уставших здесь.

—18 февраля 1984

21.

On the other side of the door: "Telegram for you"—
Whatever it is—open up!

Like holy fools before churches—
Whose prophet's words are they rasping?

Will the appointed ship, the one that's taken
so long, sear you when your eyes
rest on its sails?

In the longest minutes of fate
we don't know what awaits us.
It's not for us to see,
but all the more firmly to face,
insisting out loud on the miracle,
allotted the two of us.
According to the order of things! By right of blood!
And by every separate sigh!
And by every night without shelter!
And by delirium set to the rattle of wheels!
Not recompense and not retribution
but severest wonders,
so they go into song,
leaving the weary here.

—18 February 1984

22.

Моему незнакомому другу Дэвиду Мак Голдену

Над моей половиной мира
Распускают хвосты кометы.
На моей половине века—
Мне в глаза—половина света.
На моей половине—ветер,
И чумные пиры без меры.
Но прожектор по лицам светит
И стирает касанье смерти.
И отходит от нас безумье,
И проходят сквозь нас печали,
И стоим посредине судеб,
Упираясь в чуму плечами.
Мы задержим ее собою,
Мы шагнем поперек кошмара.
Дальше нас не пойдет—не бойтесь
На другой половине шара!

—26 февраля 1984

22.

To My Unknown Friend, David McGolden

Over my half of the earth
comets scatter their tails—
in my half of the century
to me in my eyes—half the light.
On my half—wind,
uncountable feasts of pestilence.
But searchlights shine on these faces,
erase the touch of death.
Madness leaves us.
Sadnesses filter through
and we stand among fates
setting our shoulders to the pestilence.
We'll hold it with ourselves,
pushing across the nightmare,
it won't pass beyond us—don't be afraid
on the other half of this sphere.

—26 February 1984

23.

Сойдем с ума печальною весной,
Когда снега вздыхают об апреле,
Когда уже грозит подрыв основ
Сугробам; и камины догорели,
Когда стоит над нами Орион,
Но наплывают странные созвездья,
Когда из мира не приходят вести,
Но он такой душою одарен,
Что прорывается в молчание утрат—
С ума сойти! Какого ветра милость?
Вот так проснешься как-нибудь с утра—
И все исполнится,
Как только что приснилось.

—2 марта 1984

23.

We'll go mad in a sorrowful spring
when the snows long for April,
when loss already teethes the bottoms of snowdrifts
and stoves have burned low,
when Orion stands above us
but strange constellations rise to the surface,
when no news comes from the world,
but it is illumined by such a soul
that it penetrates the quiet of loss—
To go mad! The mercy of what wind?
You wake up one day in the morning
and all will have come about
as you've just dreamed.

                                        —2 March 1984

24.

Их пророки обратятся в ветер,
В пепел обратятся их поэты,
Им не будет ни дневного света,
Ни воды, и не наступит лето.
О, конечно, это справедливо:
Как земля их носит, окаянных!
Грянут в толпы огненные ливни,
Города обуглятся краями . . .
Что поделать—сами виноваты!
Но сложу я договор с судьбою,
Чтобы быть мне здесь
И в день расплаты
Хоть кого-то заслонить собою.

—9 марта 1984

24.

Their prophets will turn to wind,
their poets to ashes,
and there will be neither daylight nor water;
summer will not come for them.
Oh, of course, it's fair:
how the earth carries its damned!
Fiery downpours will erupt in their crowds;
cities charred to the edges . . .
What's to be done? They're the guilty ones!
But I'll make an agreement with fate,
that I will be here,
and on the day of reckoning
shield at least someone with me.

—9 March 1984

25.

Под созвездием Девы ручьи убегают в ночь—
И доносится смех, и возня весенних баталий.
Это было уже когда то давным-давно.
Кем мы были тогда, какие ветра глотали?
Эта черная легкость взмаха—каким крылом?
Этот шалый бег по остолбеневшим водам,
Этот странный озноб (апрель, и уже светло),
Эта получужая кровь—другого кого-то—
Затаилась—а вдруг взбурлит, понесет конем—
Не удержишь изодранных губ ни уздой, ни гневом!
И тогда, ничего не успев, лишь рукой взмахнем,
Но рука—уже не рука, и хохочет Дева.

—17 марта 1984

25.

Under the constellation of the Virgin, brooks race into night—
And laughter carries to us, and the racket
of springtime battles.
It happened once—long, long ago.
Who were we then, what winds did we gulp?
Black lightness of strokes—on what wing?
That mad flight across paralyzed waters,
strange shivering (it's April and already light),
that half-alien blood—of some other someone—
concealed itself—and suddenly will surge, will bolt like a steed—
Bridles can't restrain torn lips, nor anger!
And then, having succeeded in nothing, we'll only wave a hand,
but that hand's no longer a hand, and Virgo gives a laugh.

—17 March 1984

26.

Лилии да малина,
Горностаи, белые псы,
Да знамена в размахах львиных,
Да узорчатые зубцы.
По настилам гремят копыта,
Вороненная сталь тепла.
И слетает кудрявый свиток
С перерубленного стола.
А с небес—знаменья да рыбы,
Чьи-то крылья и голоса.
Громоздятся в соборы глыбы,
Но пророки ушли в леса.
Рук иудиных отпечатки
На монетах—не на сердцах.
Но отравленные перчатки
Дарят девочкам во дворцах.

—12 апреля 1984

26.

Lilies and raspberries,
ermines, white hounds,
banners a lionsbreadth.

And figured merlons,
hoofs resound on the planking,
warm the harrowed metal-work.

An ornate scroll
falls from the hewn table
and from the heavens—signs and fishes,

someone's wings and voices.
Boulders loom above cathedrals
but the prophets have left for the forests.

The impression of Judas's hands
on coins—not hearts.
But poisoned gloves

are given to girls in the palaces.

—12 April 1984

27.

И предадут, и тут же поцелуют—
Ох, как старо! Никто не избежал.
Что ж, первый век! Гуляй напропалую,
Не отпускай потомков с кутежа!
Весенний месяц нисан длится, длится—
Ночных садов мучительный балет.
Что поцелуй? Пустая небылица.
Все скоро кончится. За пару тысяч лет.
Но этот месяц—на котором круге?—
Дойдет до нас, и прочих оттеснят,
И скажут—нам:—Пойдем умоем руки,
Мы ни при чем. Ведь все равно казнят.

—20 апреля 1984

27.

They will betray you, and then
they'll kiss you—
Oh, how ancient! No one's escaped.
Well, then, first century! Revel to your fill!
Don't release your children from the orgy!
Spring month of Nisan goes on and on—
torturous ballet of nocturnal gardens.
What, a kiss? An empty fable.
All will be over soon. In a few thousand years.
But this month—on what spin?
will reach up to us, pushing aside the others,
and they'll say—to us: —Let's go wash our hands.
We've nothing to do with it. They'll execute all the same.

—20 April 1984

28.

Так закат воспален, что не тронь!
Ну так что же?
В общем, все хорошо. А детали—
Ну что же детали . . .
Мы давно не от мира газет
Да словес, прилипающих к коже,
Да Иудиных цен.
Даже страхи—и те растеряли.
Мы давно отмолчали допросы,
Прошли по этапу,
Затвердили уроки потерь—
Чтоб ни слез и ни звука!
Мы упрямо живем—
Как зверек, отгрызающий лапу,
Чтоб уйти от капкана на трех,—
Мы освоили эту науку.
И с отважной улыбкой—
Так раны бинтуют потуже—
Мы на наши сомненья
Печальные ищем ответы—
А на наши печали—найдется трава . . .
Почему же
Так закат воспален,
Что глаза не сомкнуть до рассвета?

—22 апреля 1984

28.

The sunset is so inflamed, *don't touch!*
Well then, how goes it?
In general, all's well. As for details—
well, what of details . . .
We are long from the world of newspapers,
and of verbiage that sticks to the skin,
and of prices of Judases.
Even fears—even those, we've lost.
We long ago silenced interrogations,
passed through transport,
memorized the lessons of loss—
so we're without tears, sound.
We live stubbornly—
like a small beast who's gnawed off his paw
to get out of the trap on three—
we've mastered that science.
And with brave smile—
that way the wounds are bandaged tighter—
Our doubts—
we look for the sad answers—
and our sadness—a grass will be found . . .
Why is it
the sunset's so inflamed,
can't close my eyes till dawn?

—22 April 1984

29.

Мандельштамовской ласточкой
Падает к сердцу разлука,
Пастернак посылает дожди,
А Цветаева—ветер.
Чтоб вершилось вращенье вселенной
Без ложного звука,
Нужно слово—и только поэты
За это в ответе.
И раскаты весны пролетают
По тютчевским водам,
И сбывается классика осени
Снова и снова.
Но ничей еще голос
Крылом не достал до свободы,
Не исполнил свободу,
Хоть это и русское слово.

—25 апреля 1984

29.

Like Mandelstam's swallow
parting sinks to the heart,
Pasternak sends rains,
and Tsvetaeva—wind.
So the rotation of the universe
will be accomplished without false sound
a word is needed—and only poets
answer for that.
And the thundercracks of spring
sail by Tiutchev's waters,
and the ideal of autumn comes into being
again and again.
Yet no one's voice has reached
its wing to freedom,
rendered freedom,
though that is a Russian word.

—25 April 1984

30.

Этот вечер для долгой прогулки.
Серый час, как домашняя кошка,
Теплой тенью скользит у колена,
А подъезды печальны и гулки.
Ты надень свою старую куртку.
Мы набьем леденцами карманы
И пойдем, куда хочется сердцу,
Безо всякого дельного плана.
По заросшим ромашкой кварталам,
Где трамвай уже больше не ходит,
Где открытые низкие окна,
Но старушек в них прежних не стало.
Так мы выйдем к знакомому дому,
И увидим на спущенной шторе
Тень хозяина, и улыбнемся:
Кто сегодня в гостях, с кем он спорит?
Мы замедлим шаги: не зайти ли?
Но заманят нас сумерки дальше,
Уведут, как детишек цыгане,
Как уже много раз уводили.
И тогда, заблудившись, как дети,
В незнакомом обоим предместье,
Вдруг очнемся: мы живы и вместе!
И вернемся домой на рассвете.

—2 июля 1984

30.

This evening is made for a long walk.
Gray hour, like a housecat, glides as a warm shadow
around our knees; doorways are sad,
resonating emptiness.
Put on your old jacket. We'll fill our pockets
with sugar drops, set off wherever the heart
desires, without any plan at all,
through quarters overgrown with camomile,
where trams no longer pass,
where there are low
open windows
but the old women
who used to be at them
are gone.

Then we'll come to a familiar house,
see the shadow on the lowered shade,
the man who lives there, we'll
smile, who's visiting today?
Who's he arguing with?
We'll slow our pace:
should we drop in?

But the twilight will lure
us farther, lead us astray,
as gypsies steal little ones,
as it's led us
away so many times before.
And then having gotten lost
like children in a far-out part
neither knows, we'll suddenly
realize: we're alive and together!
And return home at dawn.

—2 July 1984

71

31.

Переменился ветер,
А новый самодержавен.
Небо встало осадой
И пригороды берет.
За северною стеною
Раскатом кони заржали,
Но первый поток прорвался
Сквозь брешь восточных ворот.
И сразу в дымном провале
Исчезли остатки башен,
Смело надвратную церковь,
Кресты и колокола.
Мой город сопротивлялся,
Он был прекрасен и страшен.
Он таял в ревущем небе,
Затопленный им дотла.
А позже, когда над нами
Сомкнулись тучи и воды,—
Никто не знал их победы
И не воспел зари.
И нет им с тех пор покоя:
Все лепят, лепят кого-то—
То руку, то край одежды,
Бессильные повторить.

—2 июля 1984

31.

The wind has shifted,
a new one has dominion.
The sky has risen like a siege wall
and holds the outskirts.
Beyond the north wall:
bellow of horses' neighing,
but the first stream has broken
through the gap in the eastern gates.
And instantly, in the smoky breach,
the remains of towers have vanished—
the gateway church—
crosses and bells swept away!
My city held them back—
wondrous, terrifying,
and melted in the exploding sky,
submerged.
And later, when above us,
stormclouds and water closed in—
no one knew their victory
and no one celebrated the dawn.
And since that time there is no rest:
they go on modeling, molding someone—
first a hand, then a garment's edge,
powerless to repeat.

—2 July 1984

32.

И за крик из колодца «мама!»
И за сшибленный с храма крест,
И за ложь твою «телеграмма,»
Когда с ордером на арест,—
Буду сниться тебе, Россия!
В окаянстве твоих побед,
В маяте твоего бессилья,
В похвальбе твоей и гульбе.
В тошноте твоего похмелья—
Отчего прошибет испуг?
Все отплакали, всех отпели—
От кого ж отшатнешься вдруг?
Отопрись, открутись обманом,
На убитых свали вину—
Все равно приду и предстану,
И в глаза твои загляну!

—5 июля 1984

32.

And for the cry from the well of "Mama!"
and for the cross knocked from the cathedral,
and for your lie of "Telegram!"
when it's an order for arrest—
You will dream of me, Russia!
In the curse of your triumphs,
the toil of your impotence,
in your bragging, carousing.
The nausea of your hangover—
Why is it that fright breaks out?
All is lamented, all laid to rest—
Who is it, makes you suddenly flinch?
Fling blame at the murdered—
Deny it, weasel out with lies.
All the same, I'll come before you,
look straight in your eyes!

—5 July 1984

Все дела заброшу—
Поминайте лихом!
Сяду на трамвайчик,
Поеду к портнихам,
Чтоб захлопотали,
Как куклу, вертели,
Чтобы сшили платье
Цвета карамели!
Три мои портнихи:
Одна молодая,
Другая постарше,
А третья седая . . .
Вот они над платьем
Мудрят, как и прежде:
Первая отмерит,
Вторая отрежет,
Третья на булавки
Прикинет: любуйся!
Иголкой прихватит
И нитку откусит.
—Ишь, как засветилось!
Облако, не платье!
Надень без заботы,
Сомни на закате,
Танцуй, с кем захочешь,
Но попомни слово:
Как разлюбишь сласти—
Ты придешь к нам снова:
За вечерним платьем,
За цветом печали . . .
Проводили садом
И вслед помахали.
Месяцы ли, годы
Буду вспоминать я

33.

I'll drop all that I'm doing—
think ill of me if you want!
I'll get on a tram
and ride to the dressmakers' shop,
so they'll bustle about
turn me around like a doll
then they'll sew me a dress
the color of caramel!
My dressmakers are three:
one young,
another a bit older,
and the third gray . . .
And they'll set about cleverly
just as before
the first will measure
the second will cut
and the third will pin it
piece to piece:
See how lovely!
She'll baste it together,
bite off a thread.
Look, how it glows!
It's a cloud, not a dress!
Put it on without worry,
crease it at sunset,
dance with whomever you will!
But remember:
when you're bored with sweets
you'll come once again
for an evening dress
for the color of sadness . . .
They saw me out through the garden,
waving after.
For years I'll remember
how I was encircled

Как меня кружило
Молодое платье,
Как одна смеялась,
Одна подмигнула . . .
Почему же третья—
Седая—вздохнула?

—6 июля 1984

by the new dress—
spun round—whirling—
One laughed,
one winked . . .
Why did the third—
the gray one—sigh?

—6 July 1984

34.

Ты себя не спрашивай—поэт ли?
Не замедлят—возведут в пииты!
Все пути—от пули и до петли—
Для тебя с рождения открыты.
И когда забьется человечье—
Ты поймешь, мотив припоминая:
От Елабуги до Черной речки—
Широка страна моя родная.

—13 июля 1984

34.

Don't ask yourself—are you a poet or not?
They won't waste time—they'll raise you to poethood!
All roads—from bullet to noose—
open to you from birth.
And when it begins to beat like a human's
you'll understand, recalling the tune:
from Elabuga to Black River—
Broad is my native land.

—13 July 1984

35.

Когда-нибудь, когда-нибудь
Мы молча завершим свой путь
И сбросим в донник рюкзаки и годы.
И, невесомо распрямясь,
Порвем мучительную связь
Между собой и дальним поворотом.
И мы увидим, что пришли
К такому берегу Земли,
Что нет безмолвней, выжженней и чище.
За степью сливы расцветут,
Но наше сердце дрогнет тут:
Как это грустно—находить, что ищем!
Нам будет странно без долгов,
Доброжелателей, врагов,
Чумных пиров, осатанелых скачек.
Мы расседлаем день—пастись,
Мы удержать песок в горсти
Не попытаемся—теперь ведь все иначе.
Пускай победам нашим счет
Другая летопись ведет,
А мы свободны—будто после школы.
Жара спадает, стынет шлях,
Но на оставленных полях
Еще звенят медлительные пчелы.
Ручей нам на руки польет,
И можно будет смыть налет
Дорожной пыли—ласковой и горькой.
И в предвечерней синеве
Конь переступит по траве
К моей руке—с последней хлебной коркой.

—16 июля 1984

35.

Some day, some day
we'll silently complete our way
throw off rucksacks, years, onto sweet clover.
And straightening up weightlessly, break this tormenting tie
between ourselves and the distant turning point.
And we'll notice, we've come to such a shore of this earth,
there's nothing quieter, more scorched or pure.

Plum trees will bloom beyond the steppe
and then our hearts will tremble:
How sad it is—to find what we look for!
It will seem strange without debts,
well-wishers, enemies, feasts of pestilence, satanic steeplechases.
We'll unsaddle the day—to graze.
Won't try holding sand
in handfuls—now it's so different.
Let the score of our winnings
be kept in other chronicles
and we'll be free—as after school.

Heat will die down, the road will cool,
but on the fields we've left
sluggish bees still thrum.
A brook will come flowing over our hands,
so we'll be able to wash off the film,
road dust—tender, bitter.
And in the blueness of dusk
a steed will cross the grass
just up to my hand—with a last crust of bread.

—16 July 1984

36.

Вот их строят внизу—их со стенки можно увидеть.
(Ну, а можно и пулю в невежливый глаз получить!)
Золоченые латы (это—в Веспасиановой свите),
Гимнастерки солдат, да центурионов плащи.
Завтра эти ребята, наверно, двинут на приступ.
И, наверно, город возьмут, изнасилуют баб—
И пойдет, как века назад и вперед,—огонь да убийства.
Если спасся—счастливый раб, если нет—то судьба.
Храм, наверно, взорвут и священников перережут.
Впрочем, может, прикажут распять, сперва допросив.
Офицеры возьмут серебро, солдаты—одежду—
И потянутся пленные глину лаптями месить.
А потом запросят ставку—что делать дальше?
И связист изойдет над рацией, матерясь.
Будет послан вдоль кабеля рвущийся к славе мальчик,
Потому что шальною стрелой перешибло связь.
А другая стрела его в живот угадает.
А потом сожгут напалмом скот и дома,
Перемерят детей колесом
И стену с землей сравняют,
Но, возможно, не тронут старух, сошедших с ума.
И не тычьте в учебник: истории смертники знают—
Прохудилось время над местом казни и дало течь.
Дай вам Бог не узнать, что видит жена соляная:
Автомат ППШ или римский короткий меч?

—23 июля 1984

36.

They're forming columns down below—you can see from the wall.
(And you can get a bullet in your rude eye!)
Gilded armor (that's in Vespasian's retinue),
soldiers' field shirts, centurions' cloaks.
Probably tomorrow these boys'll move in for the kill,
take a city, rape women—
and there will follow, just as in past times and ahead—
bonfires, murders.
If you're spared—you're a happy slave, if not—that's fate.
Probably they'll storm a temple, slash priests.
Or perhaps have them crucified, question them first.
Officers will take silver, soldiers—clothes—
and prisoners will drag, kneading through clay in sandals of bast.
And they'll call headquarters—what to do next?
And a signalman will burst into obscenities over radio.
Because their connection was broken by a stray shot
they'll send a boy, straining for glory, along a cable
and another shot will get him in the belly.
And then they'll torch the cattle, houses with napalm,
measure the children with wheels of a tank,
level walls to the ground.
But maybe they won't touch the crazed old women—
and don't keep bringing up the schoolbook: the condemned
know the histories—
Time's worn thin above the place of execution, begins to leak.
God grant you don't learn what the wife of salt will see:
A PPSh machine gun or a short Roman sword?

—23 July 1984

85

37.

Я заведу большой сундук
И все сложу туда:
Картинку с грешником в аду
И сонного кота.
И карты стран, которых нет,
И шляпу-котелок,
Еще старинный пистолет,
Рогатку и свисток.
И с этим самым сундуком
Я завтра двину в путь,
И—где верхом, а где пешком—
Дойду куда-нибудь.
Пусть будет край, куда приду,
На сгибе карты стерт!
Картинкой с грешником в аду
Мы разведем костер,
Кот распугает всех зверей,
Что смотрят из кустов,
Но сахар делает добрей
Бесхвостых и с хвостом.
Мы чай заварим в котелке,
А с ним упавший лист.
Все, кто вблизи и вдалеке,
Сойдутся к нам на свист.
Мы будем песни распевать,
Болтать о сем о том,
И не загонит нас в кровать
Никто-никто-никто!
И звезды ярче леденцов
Взойдут над головой . . .
А чтоб не портить все концом,
Я не вернусь домой!

—28 июля 1984

37.

I'll take out a big trunk,
lay everything in it:
the picture of a sinner in hell,
and the sleepy cat,
and maps of countries that don't exist,
a bowler hat,
an ancient pistol too,
a whistle and slingshot.
And with the trunk
I'll be on my way,
here on horseback, there on foot—
I'll come to a place.
May the land that I reach
be erased in the crease of a map!
With the picture of a sinner in hell
we'll start a campfire,
the cat will frighten off wild beasts
who watch from behind the bushes,
but sugar will make them kinder—
those with tails and those who have none.
We'll brew tea in a pot,
and with it, the fallen leaf.
At our whistle,
all those near and far
will gather to us.
We'll sing our songs,
jabbering this and that
and won't be chased into bed
by anyone at all!
And stars brighter than beaten sugar
will rise above our heads . . .
And not to spoil it with an end,
I won't return home!

—28 July 1984

38.

Нас Россией клеймит
Добела раскаленная вьюга,
Мракобесие темных воронок
Провалов под снег.
—Прочь, безглазая, прочь!
Только как нам уйти друг от друга—
В бесконечном круженье,
В родстве и сражении с ней?
А когда наконец отобьешься
От нежности тяжкой
Самовластных объятий,
В которых уснуть—так навек,
Все плывет в голове,
Как от первой ребячьей затяжки,
И разодраны легкие,
Как нестандартный конверт.
А потом, ожидая, пока отойдет от наркоза
Все, что вышло живьем
Из безлюдных ее холодов,—
Знать, что русские ангелы,
Как воробьи на морозах,
Замерзают под утро
И падают в снег с проводов.

—4 августа 1984

38.

Russia marks us,
her blizzard scorched to whiteness,
obscurantism of dark funnels,
of crevices in snow.
—Get away, you eyeless one, away!
Only how are we to leave each other—
In endless whirling?
In discord? Kinship with her?
And when at last you beat yourself free
from the excruciating tenderness
of despotic embraces,
—for if you fall asleep it's to remain there forever—
everything swims in your head,
as young ones draw on cigarettes,
and the lungs are lacerated
like an odd-sized envelope.
And then waiting, until the anesthetic passes
from everything that has come out alive
from its unpeopled colds—
To know that Russian angels,
like sparrows in a cold snap
become frozen towards dawn
and fall to the snow from the wires.

—4 August 1984

39.

С перепоя неймется, матушка?
Отойдешь к утру, ничего!
Все мерещатся ангелы падшие?
Не впервой!
Ну-ка хлопни их туфлей сношенной,
В стенку вмажь!
Вот и будет им ров некошенный,
Дурья блажь!
Бей с размажу, лепи, что силы—
Так их мать!
Да по девкам ихним красивым,
Да по крылышкам, чтоб летать
Разучились! Да по сусалам!
По глазам!
Что ж ты валишься, мать? Устала?
Что ты взвыла? На образа
Что косишься, когда их нету?
Что ты видишь там по углам?
Ты ж очкарику прошлым летом
За поллитру их отдала!
Ну, кончай причитать, мамаша!
Раз по ангелам не попасть—
Хлопни рюмку, давай попляшем—
Наша власть!
Наше право: хотим—гуляем—
Раззудись плечо!
Что ж ты ткнулась в подол соплями?
Ну, о чем?
Что ты пялишься, как на Каина?
Спать пора!

39.

Drinking's set you reeling, matushka?
You'll recover towards morning, it's nothing!
Still fancy you see fallen angels?
That's not the first time!
Well, smack at them with a worn out shoe,
smear them to the wall!
There's an unmown ditch for them,
such foolishness!
Strike with all your might! Crack 'em one—
that's it, you mother!
And get at their pretty girls,
and their gauzy
wings, *may they
forget to fly*!
And their fat mugs!
And their eyes!
How come you're falling, mother? Tired?
Why the howl? How come you squint
at images when none are here?
What do you see in those corners?
You know you unloaded the icons last summer
to the fellow in spectacles
for a half-liter!
Stop wailing, mamasha!
If you can't get at those angels—
toss down a glass, let's have a dance—
if we please!
It's our privilege: if we want—we fool around,
give in to the itch!
How come you're sniveling on your hem?
What's the matter?
How come you're staring, as if at Cain?
Time to sleep!

Нет, теперь поехала каяться.
Это точно, что до утра.

—4 августа 1984

No, now she's starting to repent.
Sure to keep her till morning.

—4 August 1984

40.

Скоро будет прилив,
Сгонит отару вод
Северный ветер,
Сдвинутся корабли.
Небо вкось поплывет.
Что случится на свете?
Выгнется линзой свод,
Хрупкий взметнут балет
Птицы-чаинки.
Выступит мед из сот,
И покачнутся в земле
Чьи-то личинки.
Дети чужих зверей
Стиснут в мехах сердца—
Шорох по норам . . .
Ветер, то ли свирель—
Не угадать лица—
Будет, и скоро.
Знают сверчки небес
Рации всех судов,
Пеленг сосновый.
Нордом сменится Вест.
Смоется след водой.
Ступишь ли снова?

—5 августа 1984

40.

Tomorrow the waters will rise,
a north wind
will drive off the flock of waters,
ships will begin to move.
The sky will sail
obliquely by. What will happen in this world?
The firmament will come to an arch
as if it were bent by a lens,
birds—tea leaves
will flutter a fragile ballet.
Honey will appear from honeycombs,
and someone's larvae
will stir in the earth.
The offspring of strange wild animals
will clench their hearts inside their furs—
a rustle spreads across the burrows . . .
wind, or else a reed flute—
One can't divine the face;
it will happen and soon.
The crickets of the heavens
know the radios of all ships,
the bearings of the pines.
The Westwind will shift to Northwind.
All trace will be washed by water.
Should one step out again?

—5 August 1984

41.

Есть праздник любования луной,
Так сказано в одной японской книге.
Подставить лоб под голубые блики,
Когда—не помню.
Кажется, весной.
А может, осенью, когда дозреет небо?
Как знать? В моем неласковом краю
Такое действо—невидаль и небыль,
Наверное, поэтому стою—
Привычно вопреки—
И жду минуты,
Когда взойдет
И медленной рукой
Погладит лоб,
И снизойдет покой
Со вкусом снега, вечера и руты.
Так мало между нами—лишь забор,
Сигнализация, два ряда заграждений
(Но не под током, кажется),
Да тени,
Которые свое происхожденье
Никак не прояснили до сих пор.
Еще решетка. Долго ли взойти,
Из проржавевших яростных колючек
Заботливо выпутывая лучик,
Неосторожно сбившийся в пути!
Оставь земле ее докучный хлам,
Не обижайся на ее игрушки!
Давай-ка лучше из помятой кружки
Хлебнем воды за то, что ты взошла!
Теперь иди, срывая облака—
Все дерзостней, все звонче, все нежнее,—
Иди, с дыханьем каждым хорошея,—
Как девочка на первых каблуках!
Теперь постой.

41.

There's a festival of adoration of the moon—
so it says in a Japanese book.
To offer one's brow under pale blue patches of light—
when—I don't remember.
In spring, it seems.
But maybe in autumn, when the sky ripens?
How can you know? In my cold territory
such pageant's a fable, a fairy tale;
probably that's why I stand
habitually contrary—
and wait for the minute
when it will rise
and slowly with its hand
stroke my brow,
and peace will descend
with the taste of snow, evening, rue.
So little lies between us—a fence,
signal apparatus, two rows of barriers
(not electrified, it seems),
and shadows
whose source they have not yet managed
to clarify.
A grate too. Will it take long to rise
through rusted fierce spikes, lovingly extricating a ray
that's carelessly lost its way?
Leave her riffraff to the earth,
don't be offended by her toys!
Better to drink up from a crumpled mug—
to your rising!
Now go, tearing the clouds,
ever more audacious, more resonant, tender—
go, growing more beautiful with every breath—
Like a young girl on her first heels!
Now hold,

До дна зрачков согрей!
Я так хочу надолго наглядеться!
А что решетке никуда не деться—
Так сквозь решетку зрение острей.

—7 августа 1984

warm my pupils through to the depths.
I want so to look my fill, for a long time!
As for the grating that can never go away—
through a grating, vision is sharper.

—7 August 1984

Ну, так будем жить,
Как велит душа,
Других хлебов не прося.
Я себе заведу ручного мыша,
Пока собаку нельзя.
И мы с ним будем жить-поживать,
И письма читать в углу.
И он залезет в мою кровать,
Не смывши с лапок золу.
А если письма вдруг не придут—
(Ведь мало ли что в пути!)—
Он будет, серенький, тут как тут
Сердито носом крутить.
А потом уткнется в мою ладонь:
—Ты, мол, помни, что мы вдвоем!
Ну не пить же обоим нам валидол,
Лучше хлебушка пожуем!
Я горбушку помятую разверну,
И мы глянем на мир добрей.
И мы с ним сочиним такую страну,
Где ни кошек, ни лагерей.
Мы в два счета отменим там холода,
Разведем бананы в садах . . .
Может нас после срока сошлют туда,
А вернее, что в Магадан.
Но, когда меня возьмут на этап
И поведут сквозь шмон—
За мной увяжется по пятам
И всюду пролезет он.
Я его посажу в потайной карман,
Чтобы грелся под стук колес.
И мы сахар честно съедим пополам—
По 10 граммов на нос.
И куда ни проложена колея—
Нам везде нипочем теперь.

42.

Well, we'll live
as the soul directs,
not asking for other bread.
And I will get myself a tame mouse
while having a dog is impossible.
And he and I will go along,
read letters in the corner.
He'll climb into my bed
without wiping the soot from his paws.
And if letters suddenly stop—
(after all, anything could happen on the way!)—
he, the gray one, then and there,
will angrily wrinkle his nose.
And then bury himself in my palm:
as if to say, remember, we're in this together!
No need for both to take *validol*,
better to chew on a crust!
I'll bring out a crushed heel of bread,
and we'll regard the world more kindly.
He and I will invent a land
where there are neither cats nor camps.
In two strokes we'll abolish the coldness,
make bananas grow in the gardens . . .
Maybe after our term we'll be sent there,
but more likely to Magadan.
But when I'm taken for transport
and put through the search,
he'll tag along at my heels,
crawl wherever I go.
I'll set him in a secret pocket
so he'll keep warm to the rumble of wheels.
And we'll fairly go halves on sugar—
ten grams per nose.
And wherever the track is laid—
anywhere suits us now.

Мы ведь оба старые зэки—я
И мой длиннохвостый зверь.
За любой решеткой нам будет дом,
За любым февралем—весна . . .
А собаку мы все-таки заведем,
Но в лучшие времена.

—8 августа 1984

For we're both old zeks—I
and my long-tailed beast.
We'll make a home behind any bars,
beyond any February—spring . . .
We'll raise a dog anyway,
but in better times.

—8 August 1984

43.

Земляничный город

В Земляничном городе —
Звонкие окошки,
В Земляничном городе —
Молоко для кошки,
В Земляничном городе —
Пряники с картинками,
Башенки с часами,
Цыганки с корзинками,
Лужи да кораблики,
Финики — бананы,
Гордые вороны,
Мудрые бараны.
Целый вечер — мультики,
Целый день — мороженое,
А по воскресеньям —
И добавки можно!
И уже видали
В Земляничном городе
Выраженье счастья
У лошади на морде!
А еще там ежики,
Тигры и медведи!
Купим кучу сахару —
И скорей поедем
В Земляничный город!

43.

Wildstrawberry Town

In Wildstrawberry Town—
clear-ringing little windows,
in Wildstrawberry Town—
milk for the cat,
in Wildstrawberry Town—
gingerbread with pictures,
towers with clocks,
gypsies with baskets,
puddles and boats,
figs and bananas,
haughty crows,
wise lambs.
All evening—cartoons,
all day—ice cream,
and on Sundays—
second helpings!
They've even recorded
in Wildstrawberry Town—
expressions of happiness
on the face of a horse!
Hedgehogs too,
tigers and bears!
Let's buy heaps of sugar—
set off without cares
to Wildstrawberry town.

44.

Подумаешь — сгрызли метлу от ступы
И полподметки от сапога!
У нас, драконов, чешутся зубы
По полнолуниям и четвергам!
Ну скушали грабли — большое дело!
Сожрали осла — велика печаль!
Моя бабуся однажды съела
Министра — и то никто не кричал.
А что мы съели — то съели честно:
Интриги-сплетни нам не с руки.
Уж если что-то чесать — известно,
Что лучше зубы, чем языки.
Нам все годится: хрум-хрум — и нету!
Вот только было бы чем запить.
Сжуем и туфельку, и карету,
А Золушку выплюнем — так и быть!
Но, дело имея с людской породой,
Мотайте, мальчики, на усы:
Я дожил до старости тем, что сроду
Не ел их докторской колбасы.
Да, мы жуем, но рискуем сами —
Такая уж наша драконья жисть!
Ох, снова, проклятые, зачесались . . .
У вас не найдется, чего погрызть?

44.

Just think—we've chewed up the broom and the kettle
and half the sole of a boot!
Our dragon's teeth itch
on Thursdays and full moons!
So we dined on rakes—no big deal!
Devoured an ass—no harm done!
My grandma once ate
a minister—no one complained!
And what we ate—we ate honestly:
Intrigues and gossip aren't our way.
If something has to itch—it's well known,
better teeth, than tongues.
We'll take anything: khrum-khrum—all gone!
If only we had something to wash it down.
We'll even chomp the slipper and coach,
but spit out Cinderella—that's how it goes.
But with the human species,
mark well, boys:
I've lived to a ripe old age since from the first
I never ate their low-grade sausage.
Yes, we chew, but at our own risk—
That's our dragonian plight!
Oh, the damned itching's started up . . .
Do you happen to have something to bite?

Лошади мои, лошади!
По каким боям — гривы по ветру?
Что за бабы плачут у повода?
Что за пули ждут своей очереди?
Серые мои, рыжие!
По каким холстам — легкой поступью?
Из каких веков, мои поздние?
Из каких переделок выжили?
Небывалые мои, гордые!
Не косите свои агатовые!
Уходя, не надо оглядываться.
Лишь копыта в небо — аккордами.

45.

Horses, my horses!
What battles—manes shaking off the wind?
What women weep, standing by the reins?
What bullets wait their turn?
Grayish ones, chestnut!
Across what canvases—stepping lightly?
Out of what centuries, my late ones?
What nets did you survive?
Peerless ones, proud ones!
Don't narrow your anthracite eyes!
As you step away, no need to look back.
In chords—just hooves into sky.

46.

O.M.

Ни сына не оставивший, ни дома,
Во вьюгу поднятый среди строки,
Щербленою дорогою ведомый —
Нелепым дуновением руки,
Бессмертным птичьим взмахом —
Не меня ли
Благословил на этот мерзлый путь?
И правящему черными конями
Я не боюсь в глазницы заглянуть:
Ни странных птиц кружение и трепет,
Ни гул последней облачной черты —
Не преуспеют испугать, раз ты
Уже на берег вышел, чтобы встретить,
И ждешь у края сумрачной воды.
Я узнаю твой взмах — и рвутся звенья
Бессильных уз, и опадает тлен!
А ты сейчас шагнешь по неземле —
И руку мне подашь, чтобы забвенье
Не доплеснуло до моих колен.

46.

To O.M.

Leaving neither son nor home,
lifted midverse into blizzard,
led along the pitted road,
by the absurd waft of a hand—
immortal bird's wingstroke—
Wasn't I blessed by him
along this frozen road?
Looking up, I'm not afraid
of his eye sockets, driver of black steeds:
or the circling commotion of strange birds,
rumbling farthest line of clouds—
They won't frighten me, since you've
already come on the shore to meet me,
waiting at the twilight water's edge.
I recognize your wave—and the links break apart—
powerless bonds—and decay falls away!
Now you'll step out onto unearth,
give me your hand so that oblivion
doesn't splash up to my knees.

47.

И — вечерний полет, по-ребячьи раскинувши руки,
Словно в бездну, роняя затылок в крахмальную стынь —
Пронесемся по снам, ни в одном не уставшие круге,
В обомлевших ветрах наводя грозовые мосты!

Мы узнаем там тех, кого вспомнить пытались, но меркла
У границы сознанья прозрачная память веков.
Мы в нее свою жизнь наводили, как встречное зеркало,
Но глаза ослеплял свет неведомых нам берегов.

В озареньи полета мы будем бесстрашны и мудры,
И придут к нам крылатые звери с небесных ворот . . .
А в кого превратимся, ударившись оземь, наутро —
Нам еще не известно, и стоит ли знать наперед?

47.

And—evening flight, spreading our arms out like children,
as if into a chasm, dropping our heads into stiff-starched cold—
we'll be carried through dreams, not tiring in a single circle,
building stormcloud bridges in stunned winds.

We'll recognize those we've tried to remember, but at edges
of consciousness the translucent memory of centuries fades.
We've turned in its direction, as if to an oncoming mirror,
but light of unfamiliar shores blinded our eyes.

In the illumination of flight we'll be fearless and wise,
and winged beasts will come towards us from heavens' gates . . .
It's still unknown, who we'll be turned to in morning,
after hitting the shore, but must one know what's ahead?

Notes to the Poems

1. "Our conscience has two inflections"

"in the alphabet there are two silent signs . . . ": The Cyrillic alphabet contains two letters termed the "hard sign" and "soft sign," which are not themselves pronounced but affect the pronunciation of adjacent letters. The hard sign, formerly the final letter of any word ending in an unpalatalized consonant (a large percentage of Russian nouns), was made virtually obsolete by the orthographic reform of 1918.

3. "For Tatyana Velikanova"

Tatyana Velikanova, a prominent human rights activist since the early 1970s, was arrested in 1979 and convicted of editing the *Chronicle of Current Events*, the Soviet human rights movement's central publication. Velikanova was sentenced to five years' imprisonment and five years' internal exile. She served the first part of that sentence in the same camp as Ratushinskaya and was a co-signatory of several appeals issued by the women prisoners. In the fall of 1983 Velikanova was released from the camp to begin her term of exile in Central Asia. There she has repeatedly been refused employment. As a result she is now threatened with arrest for "parasitism," despite the fact that in February 1987 she turned fifty-five, the official retirement age for women.

"with salt, not bread . . . ": Bread and salt are the traditional Russian symbols of hospitality and good will.

4. "Some tomorrow, little ship of ours, Lesser Zone"

Zone 4 of corrective labor camp number 3 at Barashevo, where Ratushinskaya was imprisoned, is the only known labor camp in the USSR for women who are "especially dangerous state criminals." The inmates referred to their zone, one of six at Barashevo, as the "small" or "lesser" zone. In unofficial Soviet parlance, the "lesser zone" is a metaphor for the whole Gulag, as opposed to the "greater zone" of the non-labor-camp Soviet Union.

6. "Give me a nickname, prison"

"so I'll be welcomed/with endearments by Kolyma . . . ": Many Soviet labor camps have been located in Kolyma, a desolate region of northeastern Siberia.

9. "Now the cries have died down, Penelope"

"She-who-separates": In folkloric usage, the *razluchnitsa* is a female figure who separates loved ones, sometimes through death.

10. "For Tanya Osipova and Vanya Kovalev"

Tatyana Osipova was arrested in 1980 for participating in the unofficial Helsinki monitoring group in Moscow. She served a five-year sentence, overlapping with Ratushinskaya at the Barashevo camp. For her active role in hunger strikes and other protests in the camp, she was given an additional two-year term. After one-and-a-half years of that term Osipova was released (at the same time as Ratushinskaya), and sent to serve a five-year term in internal exile. She has joined her husband, fellow Helsinki monitor Ivan Kovalev, who after completing a five-year labor camp term is also in internal exile. Osipova needs extensive medical treatment; both she and Kovalev wish to emigrate.

14. "I'm sitting on the floor, leaning against the radiator . . . "

"Shizo climate . . . ": *Shizo* is a special punishment and isolation cell, where prisoners were often held in conditions of extreme cold.

"Someone who resists/ in Perm's camp also doesn't sleep . . . ": Perm is a city in the Urals on the Kama River, near several labor camps where male political prisoners are held.

15. "Tanya Osipova, I've had enough of you!"

Ratushinskaya and Osipova (see note above) spent much of December 1983 in a freezing punishment cell (*shizo*); both were in need of medical treatment. They were disciplined in part for participating in a work strike to protest the denial of visits to a fellow prisoner. Both intermittently engaged in hunger strikes while in and out of *shizo*, hoping by their action to gain the release from *shizo* of Natalya Lazareva, who was critically ill.

"And where was I for you in Lefortovo": Lefortovo is a KGB detention and interrogation prison in Moscow.

16. "For Ilyusha"

The poem is dedicated to Ilya Nykin, a close friend and university classmate of Ratushinskaya's who emigrated from the Soviet Union in 1978 and now lives in the United States.

18. "Bear Song"

"little pillows,/to your little ears.": The last two lines of the English render the final Russian line, which contains a pun on the word "pillows" (*podushki*). The word's two syllables, when separated, form the phrase "to your little ears."

20. "We will not go into that river . . . "

"We'll remember conversation through walls . . . ": The Russian *razgovory v kruzhku* (literally, "conversations into a mug") refers to a means of communicating between prison cells by placing a mug against the wall and speaking through it so as to create a more resonant sound.

22. "To my Unknown Friend, David McGolden"

The addressee of this poem is a letter-writer whose supportive note reached Ratushinskaya in prison.

34. "Don't ask yourself—are you a poet or not?"

"From Elabuga to Black River . . . ": Both are places where great Russian poets met untimely deaths. Marina Tsvetaeva hanged herself in the town of Elabuga in 1941. Black River is the site, near St. Petersburg (Leningrad), of Pushkin's fatal duel with Dantes in 1837.

"*Broad is my native land*": The title and first line of a widely-sung patriotic song of the Stalinist era.

38. "Russia marks us . . . "

"Get away, you eyeless one, away!": In Russian folklore, the "eyeless one" is Death.

39. "Drinking's set you reeling, matushka?"

"You know you unloaded the icons last summer/to the fellow in spectacles . . . ": The line refers to the practice of cityfolk going to old villages to buy icons and other handicrafts (often at a fraction of their worth, as in this poem, where the price was a half-liter of vodka).

42. "Well, we'll live . . . "

"No need for both to take *validol* . . . ": "*Validol*" is a commonly-used sedative.

"Maybe after our term we'll be sent there,/ but more likely to Magadan . . . ": The administrative center of the northeast Siberian Kolyma region, Magadan has often served as a place of exile for former labor camp prisoners.

44. "Just think—we've chewed up the broom . . . "

The first line in Russian has "broom from the mortar." Baba Yaga, the witch of Russian folklore, flies standing in a giant mortar, sweeping the air with her broom.

46. "Leaving neither son nor home . . . "

The dedication is to Osip Mandelstam. Arrested in May 1938, the great poet died (according to the official record) in a transit camp in December of that year.

Chronology

1954   Irina Ratushinskaya was born in Odessa on 4 March. Her parents were registered as Russian nationals although a branch of the family was descended from Polish landed gentry.

1971   She began to study physics at the University of Odessa where the following year she had her first encounter with KGB agents who unsuccessfully attempted to recruit her.

1976   Ratushinskaya taught physics and mathematics at a secondary school; later she became an assistant lecturer at the Odessa Pedagogical Institute. In 1977 KGB officials objected to a university play which Ratushinskaya had helped to write. She was offered a post on the examination committee of the Pedagogical Institute and unofficially was advised to discriminate against Jewish applicants. When she turned down the position she was transferred to the laboratory staff and soon was dismissed. She began to feel a serious commitment to writing poetry.

1979   Ratushinskaya married Igor Gerashchenko, an engineer, and moved to Kiev.

1980   Together they applied for permission to travel abroad but visas were denied. Slowly they became active in the Soviet human rights movement and wrote their first letter on behalf of Andrei Sakharov.

1981   In August they were interrogated by KGB agents who advised them to give up their human rights activities. Ratushinskaya was told that she must stop writing poetry. In November Gerashchenko was dismissed from his job so that they had no means of support. On 10 December they were arrested during the annual demonstration in defense of human rights in Moscow's Pushkin Square and sentenced to prison for ten days.

1982   In April a toxic substance was sprayed on the door of their apartment. Ratushinskaya and Gerashchenko suffered a "mild poisoning." Their apartment was ransacked four times during the summer. They were offered jobs as farm laborers during the apple harvest but they were, in fact, being framed by the KGB. On 17 September, Ratushinskaya was arrested in the village of Lyshnya and sent to a KGB prison.

1983   On 5 March, Ratushinskaya was sentenced to seven years of hard labor to be followed by five years of internal exile. On 12 April, she was deported to the strict regime camp at Barashevo, three hundred miles southeast of Moscow.

1984   Ratushinskaya finished *Beyond the Limit* in August. Her health deteriorated as she suffered from fever, edemas, and pain in the region of the kidneys.

1985   She was placed in PKT (a prison within the labor camp) in August and remained there for over half a year. She was denied visits from relatives or friends. In the autumn the camp authorities shaved her head.

1986   The 48th International PEN congress, meeting in New York, passed a resolution calling for the release of Irina Ratushinskaya in conjunction with the release of Filipino poet and journalist Mila Aguilar as an act of clemency and a gesture for international detente and peace in the world. Arthur Miller and Vassily Aksyonov participated in a press conference addressing the subject of her imprisonment. In the spring, concurrent demonstrations and poetry readings were held on her behalf in London, New York, and Chicago. Ratushinskaya was transported to Kiev in July and remained in a KGB prison where authorities pressed her to sign a self-incriminating statement. In September there were demonstrations on her behalf in cities all over Europe and the United States. On 9 October, one day before the

Reykjavik Summit, she was released from prison. In November, Ratushinskaya and Gerashchenko applied for visas to travel abroad and they were denied but in December the decision was reversed. On 17 December, Ratushinskaya and Gerashchenko traveled to London.